CONTENTS

INTRODUCTION

A 17th-century design that originated in France, a French door is basically a window that usually comes in a pair. Over the years, its use has evolved beyond its original function as a light door. The trend eventually reached the kitchen appliance industry, starting with refrigerators.

Recently, French door styles have also gained popularity in ovens, including convection and countertop models. The design provides a more ergonomic design and easy access to cooked food, with the doors opening to both sides instead of dropping down.

In 1914, the first oven that uses a fan to radiate heat inside was invented. But it wasn't until 1945 that a commercial model was made available in the market for the first time.

Over the years, countertop convection ovens gained popularity as the demand for space-saving appliances grew. Multifunctionality and kid friendliness also adds to the appeal of countertop models over larger ovens.

What is Oster Digital French Door Oven?

The Oster Digital French Door Oven is an elegant countertop convection oven. It features an attractive and unique two-door design that opens with a single pull. Et voilà! That's one less hassle for meal preparation.

How Does It Work?

The Oster Digital French Door Oven uses a turbo convection baking technology. Cooking is made more efficient with the help of a built-in fan. Hot air is circulated inside the oven chamber, aiding the faster cooking and browning of food. Food cooks more evenly as well.

Using this technology allows the Oster Digital French Door Oven to utilize up to half the energy required with other conventional cooking methods.

Various Functions

With its large exterior, the Oster Digital French Door Oven provides plenty of space to cook full meals at once.

Convection cook, bake, broil, dehydrate, defrost, warm food, or make pizza by selecting the corresponding function on the control panel.

The dehydrate function has a preset temperature of 150 degrees F to slowly cook the food with an adjustable time of up to 6 hours.

Setting the temperature and cooking time is also convenient with the digital control panel. The unit's preheat setting allows the oven to reach the temperature required for precise cooking.

The timer can be set up to 90 minutes, and it will turn the oven off automatically once the required cooking time has been reached.

The Oster Digital French Door's clear tempered glass doors make it easy to view the food. An interior light makes it even more convenient to check on the food, as well.

The two removable wire racks for grilling and broiling, and the 2-in-1 baking pan and cookie sheet for baking are all made of durable materials. Use the rack and pan together to function as a broiling pan.

The unit also comes with a removable pull-out crumb tray for easy clean-up.

Tips for Usage

Before using your Oster Digital French Door Oven for the first time, make sure to remove all the stickers on the surface as the oven can get very hot when in operation. Also, remove all paper or documents inside the oven to avoid fire.

Clean the removable components and then dry thoroughly before using. Never set the unit on a wooden surface. Not all surfaces and countertops can withstand the heat generated by ovens. Always use a trivet or hot [ad under your oven to prevent possible damage to the countertop.

Place the Oster Digital French Door Oven on a flat and stable surface near a 120 Volt AC electrical outlet. Allow at least 6 inches of clearance space between the unit and other surfaces or cords.

Set the unit at the highest temperature and let it run for about 5 minutes. A slight smell and smoke are normal.

Where to place the oven rack depends on the desired level of browning and the size of the food to cook. To prevent burning on the top or bottom, adjust the rack accordingly. The upper rack guide is best for toasting.

The ideal pan positioning, on the other hand, will depend on the cooking function. Never use the broil pan under the rack when in the lower position. For grilling or broiling, place the pan under the rack.

Place the pan on top of the rack if the oven is set to baking.

Matters That Need Attention

After the first use, a burnt smell can be an indication of food build-up in the crumb tray, on the heating elements, or elsewhere inside the oven.

An incorrect time or temperature setting, and rack placement are factors to consider when coming up with undercooked or overcooked foods.

The selected function setting determines which heating element will heat up while cooking. If you notice that only one heating element is operating, check if the oven is set to warm or broil function.

Likewise, check the function setting if both heating elements are off. To maintain proper heat, the heating elements cycle through on and off during the cooking period.

Be careful when pulling the rack out of the oven as the rack tends to tilt downward and may cause the hot food to shift or even spill out.

Always handle the metal rack and cooked food with care. They can be very hot.

Cleaning & Maintenance

Aside from regular clean-up, the Oster Digital French Door Oven does not require any further maintenance.

Make sure the oven is turned off and unplugged before attempting to clean it. As with other kitchen appliances, it is ideal to clean your Oster Digital French Door Oven with each use after letting it cool down for a few minutes.

Cleaning is especially important when you intend to keep your oven in storage for long periods. Always store your Oster Digital French Door Oven on a dry and stable surface.

The oven features easy-to-clean interior walls for fast clean-up. No need for scrubbing brushes, abrasive cleaners, and strong chemicals. All of these will only potentially damage the coating of your oven. Instead, use a moist cloth with mild soapy water to wipe the surface and interior of the unit where needed.

Pull out the removable crumb tray to dispose of food crumbs to avoid accumulations.

Wipe the removable wire rack and baking pan or wash them in the dishwasher.

Remember to thoroughly dry the unit right away. Never immerse the unit in water.

Cooking Timetable

In general, countertop ovens heat faster than regular ovens and require shorter cooking times. You may need to adjust the temperature and timer to get the desired results. Changing rack positions halfway through cooking will also help.

For example, you might need to cook pizzas for about one-half the recommended time, and then switch the rack positions to evenly cook the top and bottom of the pizza.

Most of the time, shortening the cooking time works best. It will be easier to adjust the cooking period as needed.

Don't worry if it sounds complicated. The recipes in this cookbook will help you gain confidence in striking a balance for cooking with your Oster Digital French Door Oven. Over time, you will be able to cook just about any food as you wish.

CHAPTER 1: BRUNCHES 8 RECIPES
Sausage & Egg Casserole

Mornings don't have to be stressful when you can create hassle-free brunch dishes like this one.

Prep Time and Cooking Time: 1 hour | Serves: 12

Ingredients to Use:

- 12 oz. pork sausage, crumbled

- 1 onion, chopped

- 2 cups milk

- 2 eggs, beaten

- 4 egg whites, beaten

- 2 cups cheddar cheese, shredded

- 8 slices white bread, sliced into cubes

- 1 ½ teaspoons ground mustard

- Salt and pepper to taste

Step-by-Step Directions

1.   In a pan over medium heat, cook onion and sausage for 5 minutes, stirring often.

2.   Drain and let cool.

3.   In a bowl, whisk together milk, eggs and egg whites.

4.   Stir in the sausage mixture along with the rest of the ingredients.

5.   Pour mixture into a baking pan.

6. Place the baking pan inside the Oster Digital French Door Oven.

7. Press bake setting.

8. Set temperature to 350 degrees F.

9. Press start.

10. Cook for 40 minutes.

Serving Suggestion: Let cool for 5 minutes before slicing and serving.

Tip: Use reduced-fat sausage.

Peanut Butter & Jelly French Toast

This is the kind of brunch that you'd want to eat all day long.

Prep Time and Cooking Time: 30 minutes | Serves: 4

Ingredients to Use:

- ¼ cup peanut butter
- ¼ cup jelly
- 8 slices sandwich bread
- 2 eggs
- ¼ cup milk
- 2 tablespoons butter

Step-by-Step Directions

1. Spread a layer of peanut butter on top of the bread.
2. Top with the jelly.
3. Stack together two bread slices to create a sandwich.
4. In a bowl, beat eggs and milk.
5. Brush top side of bread with butter.
6. Dip sandwich in egg mixture.
7. Place the sandwiches inside the Oster Digital French Door Oven.
8. Choose toast setting.
9. Select shade option.
10. Press start.
11. Wait until toasting is done.

Serving Suggestion: Top with fresh strawberries and sprinkle with confectioners' sugar.

Tip: Use creamy natural peanut butter.

Italian Eggs Benedict with Pesto

Add a twist of Italian flair to your favorite eggs Benedict.

Prep Time and Cooking Time: 30 minutes | Serves: 4

Ingredients to Use:

- ½ cup butter
- 1 tablespoon pesto
- 4 egg yolks
- 1 tablespoon lemon juice
- 2 tablespoons water
- 2 teaspoons white vinegar
- 4 slices Italian bread
- 8 slices deli ham
- 4 fresh basil leaves
- 4 slices tomato
- 4 eggs, poached

Step-by-Step Directions

1. Add butter to a pan over medium heat.
2. Heat through until melted.
3. Add pesto.
4. Heat through for 2 minutes and set aside.
5. In a double boiler with simmering water, cook egg yolks, lemon juice and water.
6. Cook while stirring until mixture is thick.
7. Reduce heat and add pesto butter, stirring often.
8. Top Italian bread with deli ham, basil leaves, tomatoes and poached eggs.

9.   Place inside the Oster Digital French Door Oven.

10.   Press toast setting.

11.   Choose shade option.

12.   Select start.

13.   Wait for bread to be toasted.

14.   Drizzle with the pesto sauce and serve.

Serving Suggestion: Serve with lettuce salad.

Tip: You can also make your own pesto if you like.

Sweet Potatoes

Power up your morning with this healthy and delicious brunch dish.

Prep Time and Cooking Time: 1 hour and 15 minutes | Serves: 4

Ingredients to Use:

- 4 sweet potatoes
- 1 medium apple, chopped
- ½ cup Greek yogurt
- ¼ cup coconut flakes, toasted

Step-by-Step Directions

1. Select bake setting in your Oster Digital French Door Oven.
2. Preheat it to 400 degrees F.
3. Press start.
4. Add sweet potatoes to a baking pan.
5. Place it inside the oven.
6. Cook for 1 hour.
7. Take the sweet potatoes out of the oven.
8. Top with the apple, yogurt and coconut flakes.

Serving Suggestion: Drizzle with maple syrup.

Tip: Use coconut-flavored Greek yogurt if available.

Sausage Muffin

These sausage muffins are not only great for brunch but for snack in the afternoon or for dinner.

Prep Time and Cooking Time: 45 minutes | Serves: 4 dozen muffins

Ingredients to Use:

- 14 oz. breakfast sausages, cooked and chopped
- 2 cups all-purpose flour
- 3 teaspoons baking powder
- ¼ cup sugar
- ¼ teaspoon ground nutmeg
- ½ teaspoon ground cinnamon
- 1 teaspoon salt
- 2 cups milk
- 1 egg, beaten
- 2 tablespoons honey
- 2 tablespoons oil

Step-by-Step Directions

1. Press bake setting.
2. Preheat your oven to 350 degrees F.
3. Spray muffin pan with oil.
4. Divide chopped sausages in muffin cups.

5.   Mix the remaining ingredients in a bowl.

6.   Pour batter into the muffin cups.

7.   Place muffin pan inside the Oster Digital French Door oven. Set time to 20 minutes.

Serving Suggestion: Serve with honey or maple syrup.

Tip: You can freeze cooled baked muffins and then reheat when ready to serve.

Beef & Tortilla Bake

Here's another irresistible baked recipe for a delightful brunch.

Prep Time and Cooking Time: 50 minutes | Serves: 6

Ingredients to Use:

- 8 oz. ground beef
- ½ cup canned diced tomatoes
- 6 corn tortillas
- 2 green onions, chopped
- ½ cup Monterey Jack cheese, shredded
- ¼ cup pepper jack cheese, shredded
- 6 eggs
- ¾ cup milk
- ¾ teaspoon paprika
- ¼ teaspoon ground cumin

Step-by-Step Directions

1. Choose bake setting in your Oster Digital French Door Oven.

2. Preheat it to 350 degrees F.

3. In a pan over medium heat, cook sausage for 5 minutes, stirring often. Add tomatoes.

4. Cook for 2 more minutes.

5. Line a pie pan with tortillas.

6.   Top with the sausage mixture, green onions and cheeses.

7.   In a bowl, mix the remaining ingredients.

8.   Pour this on top of the layers.

9.   Place inside the oven.

10.   Press start. Bake for 30 minutes.

11.   Let cool for 10 minutes before slicing into wedges.

Serving Suggestion: Serve with salsa and sour cream.

Tip: Use lean ground beef.

Egg & Cheeseburger Slider

You can't go wrong with these amazingly simple slider recipe.

Prep Time and Cooking Time: 50 minutes | Serves: 6

Ingredients to Use:

- 1 lb. lean ground beef
- Salt and pepper to taste
- 8 eggs
- ½ cup water
- 12 tomato slices
- 1 cup Havarti cheese, shredded
- 12 dinner rolls, sliced in half

Step-by-Step Directions

1. Season beef with salt and pepper.
2. Form patties from the mixture.
3. In a pan over medium heat, cook the burgers for 3 minutes per side.
4. In a bowl, beat eggs and stir in water.
5. Season with salt and pepper.
6. Cook eggs in pan until set.
7. Assemble the sliders by adding patties, tomatoes and cheese to the dinner rolls.

8. Add these to the Oster Digital French Door Oven.

9. Select toast setting.

10. Choose shade option.

11. Press start.

12. Wait until it's done.

Serving Suggestion: Serve with ketchup, onions and pickles.

Tip: Use lean ground beef.

French Toast Bake with Maple & Bacon

It doesn't matter what day of the week it is, this will surely brighten up your day.

Prep Time and Cooking Time: 5 hours | Serves: 12

Ingredients to Use:

- 8 cups bread, sliced into cubes
- 2 cups
- ½ teaspoon ground cinnamon
- ¼ cup maple syrup
- ½ cup brown sugar
- 1 lb. bacon strips, cooked crisp and crumbled

Step-by-Step Directions

1. Spread bread cubes in a baking pan.
2. In a bowl, beat eggs and milk.
3. Stir in cinnamon, syrup and sugar.
4. Pour mixture on top of bread.
5. Sprinkle bacon on top.
6. Cover and refrigerate for 4 hours.
7. Place the baking pan inside the Oster Digital French Door.
8. Choose bake setting.
9. Cook at 350 degrees F.

10.   Press start.

11.   Bake for 50 minutes.

12.   Select stop.

13.   Press broil setting.

14.   Press start.

15.   Cook for 1 minute.

Serving Suggestion: Let sit for 5 minutes before slicing and serving.

Tip: Let casserole come to room temperature for 30 minutes before baking.

CHAPTER 2: BEEF, PORK & LAMB 8 RECIPES

Broiled Beef & Broccoli

Mushrooms make this broiled beef and broccoli dish even more delicious.

Prep Time and Cooking Time: 30 minutes | Serves: 8

Ingredients to Use:

- ¼ cup toasted sesame oil

- ¼ cup soy sauce

- 1 tablespoon ginger, grated

- 3 cloves garlic, minced

- 1 tablespoon brown sugar

- 2 ½ lb. flank steak

- 2 cups mushrooms, sliced

- 4 cups broccoli florets

- 2 tablespoons olive oil

Step-by-Step Directions

1. Combine sesame oil, soy sauce, ginger, garlic and sugar in a bowl.

2. Take ¼ cup from the mixture and set aside.

3. Add steak to the remaining mixture.

4. Toss mushrooms and broccoli in olive oil.

5. Spread these in a baking pan.

6. Place the baking pan on top of the broil rack inside the Oster Digital French Door Oven.

7. Select broil setting.

8. Set it to 375 degrees F.

9. Broil for 10 minutes

10. Press start.

11. Wait for cooking cycle to complete.

12. Add steak to the baking pan.

13. Drizzle with the reserved marinade.

14. Set time to 10 minutes, flipping once.

Serving Suggestion: Let steak rest for 10 minutes before slicing and serving.

Tip: Use shiitake mushrooms for this recipe.

Broiled Sirloin Steak

Tender and juicy, this broiled sirloin steak won't leave you wanting.

Prep Time and Cooking Time: 30 minutes | Serves: 4

Ingredients to Use:

- 2 tablespoons lime juice
- 1 teaspoon garlic powder
- 1 teaspoon onion powder
- ¼ teaspoon dried thyme
- ¼ teaspoon dried oregano
- ¼ teaspoon ground mustard
- 4 sirloin steaks
- 1 cup fresh mushrooms, sliced

Step-by-Step Directions

1. Mix lime juice, garlic powder, onion powder, thyme, oregano and mustard.

2. Rub mixture on both sides of steaks.

15. Add steaks and mushrooms to the broil rack inside the Oster Digital French Door Oven.

16. Select broil option.

17. Set it to 375 degrees F.

18. Set it to 8 minutes.

19. Press start.

20. Wait for cycle to complete.

Serving Suggestion: Garnish with chopped scallions.

Tip: Steaks should be at least 5 ounces each.

Russian Baked Beef

Here's how you prepare beef the Russian way.

Prep Time and Cooking Time: 1 hour and 15 minutes | Serves: 6

Ingredients to Use:

- Cooking spray
- 2 lb. beef tenderloin, sliced into strips
- Salt and pepper to taste
- 2 onions, sliced
- 1 ½ cups cheddar cheese, grated
- 3 tablespoons mayonnaise
- 1 cup milk

Step-by-Step Directions

1. Select bake function in your Oster Digital French Door Oven.
2. Preheat it to 350 degrees F.
3. Spray your baking pan with oil.
4. Add to the baking pan.
5. Season with salt and pepper.
6. Sprinkle onion and cheese on top.
7. In a bowl, mix mayo and milk.
8. Add mixture on top of cheese.
9. Set baking pan inside the oven.
10. Set it to 1 hour.
11. Press start.
12. Wait for cooking cycle to complete.

Serving Suggestion: Serve with salad and potatoes.

Tip: Slice steak across the grain.

Broiled Pork Chops with Mango Sauce

This unique pork chop recipe will surely wow everyone who gets a taste of it.

Prep Time and Cooking Time: 30 minutes | Serves: 4

Ingredients to Use:

- ¼ cup chicken broth
- 3 mangoes, sliced into cubes
- ½ teaspoon ground coriander
- 2 tablespoons apricot preserves
- 4 butterflied pork chops
- 2 teaspoons lemon pepper seasoning

Step-by-Step Directions

1. Add broth and blender in a food processor.
2. Blend until smooth.
3. Transfer to a pan over medium heat.
4. Stir in coriander and apricot preserves.
5. Bring to a boil.
6. Reduce heat and simmer for 10 minutes.
7. Season pork chops with lemon pepper seasoning.
8. Add pork chops to the broil rack inside Oster Digital French Door Oven.

9.   Press broil setting.

10.   Set it to 375 degrees F.

11.   Broil for 5 minutes per side.

12.   Serve with mango sauce.

Serving Suggestion: Garnish with herbs.

Tip: Use boneless pork chops.

Beef Curry

You don't have to go to a restaurant when you can cook something as amazing as this.

Prep Time and Cooking Time: 45 minutes | Serves: 4

Ingredients to Use:

- Salt and pepper to taste
- ½ teaspoon ground allspice
- 1 teaspoon ground cardamom
- 2 lb. beef chuck roast, sliced into cubes
- 1 tablespoon olive oil
- 2 onions, chopped
- 1 tablespoon ginger, grated
- 2 cloves garlic, minced
- 2 teaspoons curry powder
- 1 teaspoon ground cumin
- 10 oz. spinach
- ¾ cup Greek yogurt

Step-by-Step Directions

1. Mix salt, pepper, allspice and cardamom in a bowl.
2. Toss beef in spice mixture.
3. In a pan over medium heat, add oil and cook meat.
4. Transfer meat to a baking pan.
5. Add onion to the pan.
6. Cook for 4 minutes.
7. Stir in the rest of the ingredients except yogurt.
8. Cook for 3 minutes.

9. Transfer mixture to the baking pan and stir.

10. Place it inside the Oster Digital French Door Oven.

11. Select bake setting.

12. Set it to 350 degrees F.

13. Set it to 1 hour.

14. Press start.

15. Wait for cycle to complete.

16. Stir in yogurt and serve.

Serving Suggestion: Serve with hot white rice and additional yogurt.

Tip: You can also use lamb meat for this recipe.

Broiled Pork Chops

These broiled pork chops are particularly special and worth the time and effort.

Prep Time and Cooking Time: 40 minutes | Serves: 6

Ingredients to Use:

- ¾ cup water
- ¾ cup ketchup
- 2 teaspoons brown sugar
- 1 tablespoon Worcestershire sauce
- 2 tablespoons vinegar
- ½ teaspoon chili powder
- ½ teaspoon paprika
- Salt and pepper to taste
- 6 pork chops

Step-by-Step Directions

1. In a pan over medium heat, add all ingredients except pork chops.
2. Simmer sauce for 5 minutes, stirring often.
3. Brush pork chops with the sauce.
4. Place pork chops in the broil rack of the Oster Digital French Door Oven.
5. Select broil setting.
6. Set it to 375 degrees F.
7. Press start.
8. Broil for 4 minutes per side.

Serving Suggestion: Serve with remaining sauce.

Tip: Use bone-in pork chops for this recipe.

Baked Honey Pork Chop

This is as juicy, tender and delicious as you can imagine.

Prep Time and Cooking Time: 40 minutes | Serves: 4

Ingredients to Use:

- ¼ cup honey
- 1 tablespoon mustard
- 1 tablespoon Worcestershire sauce
- 4 pork cutlets
- 1 onion, sliced into wedges
- 1 cup baby carrots, trimmed
- 4 cups baby potatoes
- 1 cup peas

Step-by-Step Directions

1. Select bake setting in your Oster Digital French Door Oven.
2. Preheat it to 400 degrees F.
3. In a bowl, mix honey, mustard and Worcestershire sauce.
4. Divide mixture into 2.
5. Brush pork with half of the mixture.
6. Toss onion, carrots and potatoes with the remaining mixture.
7. Add these to a baking pan.
8. Place the baking pan inside the oven.

9. Set it to 30 minutes.

10. Press start.

11. Once cycle is complete, sprinkle peas on top.

12.   Bake for another 5 minutes.

Serving Suggestion: Garnish with fresh thyme.

Tip: You can use either fresh or frozen peas.

Broiled Rosemary Lamb

It's not often that you cook lamb at home so when you do, make sure it's something as special as this one.

Prep Time and Cooking Time: 30 minutes | Serves: 4

Ingredients to Use:

- 4 lamb chops
- 3 tablespoons avocado oil
- Salt and pepper to taste
- 4 cloves, sliced in half
- 10 sprigs rosemary

Step-by-Step Directions

1. Coat lamb with oil.
2. Season with salt and pepper.
3. Add lamb to the broil rack inside the Oster Digital French Door Oven.
4. Sprinkle garlic and rosemary on top.
5. Select broil setting.
6. Set it to 375 degrees F.
7. Set it to 10 minutes.
8. Press start.
9. Wait for cycle to complete.

Serving Suggestion: Garnish with rosemary sprigs.

Tip: You can also use olive oil if avocado oil is not available.

CHAPTER 3: FISH & SEAFOOD 8 RECIPES
Baked Seafood

This seafood dinner would definitely turn an ordinary night into something spectacular.

Prep Time and Cooking Time: 30 minutes | Serves: 2

Ingredients to Use:

- 6 scallops
- 6 shrimp, peeled and deveined
- 2 halibut fillets
- 1 tablespoon lemon juice
- 2 tablespoons butter, melted
- ⅓ cup dry white wine
- 1 clove garlic, minced
- ½ teaspoon Old Bay seasoning
- Salt and pepper to taste

Step-by-Step Directions

1. Choose bake setting in your Oster Digital French Door Oven.
2. Preheat it to 450 degrees F.
3. Arrange the seafood in a baking pan.
4. In a bowl, combine the remaining ingredients.

5.   Pour mixture over the seafood.

6.   Set it inside the oven.

7.   Press bake.

8.   Set it to 10 minutes.

9.   Press start.

10.   Wait for cycle to finish.

Serving Suggestion: Garnish with parsley.

Tip: You can also use cod fillet for this recipe.

Broiled Tilapia with Corn & Bean Salsa

Rich and colorful, this broiled tilapia dish will surely entice anyone at the dinner table.

Prep Time and Cooking Time: 10 minutes | Serves: 4

Ingredients to Use:

- 4 tilapia fillets
- 1 tablespoon olive oil
- Salt and pepper to taste
- 10 oz. canned corn kernels, drained
- 15 oz. canned black beans, rinsed and drained
- 1 red bell pepper, chopped
- 2 tablespoons green onion, minced
- ½ cup Italian salad dressing

Step-by-Step Directions

1. Coat fish with oil and season with salt and pepper.
2. Place fish on the broil rack inside the Oster Digital French Door Oven.
3. Set it to broil.
4. Set temperature to 350 degrees F and the time to 7 minutes.
5. Press start.
6. Wait for cycle to complete.
7. While waiting, combine remaining ingredients.
8. Top fish with salsa and serve.

Serving Suggestion: Serve with fresh green salad.

Tip: You can also garnish with lime wedges.

Broiled Fish Steak

Things don't get simpler than this! But expect stellar results!

Prep Time and Cooking Time: 20 minutes | Serves: 4

Ingredients to Use:

- 4 salmon steaks
- Salt and pepper to taste
- 2 tablespoons butter, melted

Step-by-Step Directions

1. Season salmon with salt and pepper.
2. Drizzle with melted butter.
3. Add salmon to the broil rack inside your Oster Digital French Door Oven.
4. Choose broil setting.
5. Set it to 350 degrees F.
6. Set time to 5 minutes.
7. Press start.
8. Drizzle with a little more butter before serving.

Serving Suggestion: Serve with green salad.

Tip: Choose thick salmon fillet cut.

Baked Honey & Ginger Salmon

You'll definitely look like a pro in the kitchen when you come out of it with a dish like this one.

Prep Time and Cooking Time: 30 minutes | Serves: 6

Ingredients to Use:

Marinade

- 1/3 cup reduced-sodium soy sauce
- ¼ cup honey
- 1/3 cup orange juice
- 1 teaspoon garlic powder
- 1 teaspoon ground ginger
- 1 green onion, chopped

Fish

- 6 salmon fillets

Step-by-Step Directions

1. Mix marinade ingredients in a bowl.
2. Add salmon to the bowl.
3. Coat evenly with the sauce.
4. Cover and refrigerate for 30 minutes.
5. Add fish to a baking pan and place this inside the Oster Digital French Door.

6. Select bake setting.

7. Set it to 375 degrees F for 15 minutes.

8. Press start.

9. Wait for cycle to complete.

Serving Suggestion: Garnish with chopped green onion.

Tip: You can extend cooking time if fish is not flaky after 15 minutes.

Baked Fish Fillet

This may look like it's a complicated dish but surprisingly, it's very easy to make!

Prep Time and Cooking Time: 30 minutes | Serves: 4

Ingredients to Use:

- 1 teaspoon olive oil
- ¼ cup onion, chopped
- 1 clove garlic, minced
- ½ teaspoon orange zest
- 2 tablespoons parsley, minced
- 4 halibut steaks
- ¼ cup orange juice
- 1 tablespoon lemon juice
- Salt to taste
- Pinch lemon-pepper seasoning

Step-by-Step Directions

1. Add oil to a pan over medium heat.
2. Cook onion and garlic for 1 minute.
3. Stir in orange zest and parsley.
4. Add halibut to a baking pan.
5. Mix lemon juice and orange juice.

6. Pour this over the fish.

7. Sprinkle with salt and lemon pepper.

8. Top with onion mixture.

9. Place inside the Oster Digital French Door Oven.

10. Select bake setting.

11. Set it to 400 degrees F for 20 minutes.

12. Press start.

13. Wait for cycle to complete.

Serving Suggestion: Serve on a bed of carrot strips.

Tip: Check if fish is flaky enough.

Broiled Tilapia with Lemon Butter

For sure, you'll enjoy every bite of this broiled tilapia with lemon butter sauce.

Prep Time and Cooking Time: 30 minutes | Serves: 4

Ingredients to Use:

- 4 tilapia fillets
- 1 teaspoon garlic powder
- ¼ cup butter, melted
- ¼ cup soy sauce
- ¼ cup lemon juice

Step-by-Step Directions

1. Sprinkle both sides of tilapia with garlic powder.
2. In a bowl, mix butter, soy sauce and lemon juice.
3. Pour mixture over the tilapia.
4. Marinate for 10 minutes.
5. Add fish to the broil rack inside the Oster Digital French Door Oven.
6. Press broil function.
7. Set it to 400 degrees F for 5 minutes.
8. Press start.
9. Wait for cycle to complete.

Serving Suggestion: Sprinkle with paprika before serving.

Tip: Use low-sodium soy sauce.

Broiled Scallops & Shrimp

You can't find anything bad to say about this dish that is not only delicious but also very easy to make.

Prep Time and Cooking Time: 15 minutes | Serves: 6

Ingredients to Use:

- 3 cloves garlic, minced

- ¼ cup butter, melted

- 1 tablespoon lemon juice

- 1 tablespoon Worcestershire sauce

- ¼ cup dry white wine

- 1 lb. shrimp, peeled and deveined

- 1 lb. scallops

- 1 pint cherry tomatoes, sliced in half

- Salt and pepper to taste

- Pinch red pepper flakes

- 5 oz. baby spinach leaves

Step-by-Step Directions

1. Combine all the ingredients except spinach in the broil rack.

2. Set it inside the Oster Digital French Door Oven.

3. Select broil setting.

4. Set it to 400 degrees F for 5 minutes.

5.   Press start.

6.   Wait for cycle to complete.

7.   Stir in spinach.

8.   Press bake setting.

9.   Cook for 2 minutes.

Serving Suggestion: Serve with toasted French bread.

Tip: You can also use frozen shrimp for this recipe.

Baked Cod Fillet

This is one of the simplest yet most satisfying fish dish you'll ever get to try.

Prep Time and Cooking Time: 30 minutes | Serves: 4

Ingredients to Use:

- 4 cod fillets
- 3 tablespoons melted butter
- Pinch paprika
- Salt and pepper to taste

Step-by-Step Directions

1. Brush both sides of fish with butter.
2. Season it with paprika, salt and pepper.
3. Place fish inside the Oster Digital French Door Oven.
4. Select bake setting.
5. Set it to 400 degrees F for 20 minutes.
6. Press start.
7. Wait for cycle to finish.

Serving Suggestion: Serve with cucumber and tomato salad.

Tip: You can also use haddock fillet for this recipe.

CHAPTER 4: CHICKEN & POULTRY 8 RECIPES
Garlic Broiled Chicken

This is a super tasty dish that you will definitely have a lot of preparing.

Prep Time and Cooking Time: 30 minutes | Serves: 6

Ingredients to Use:

- 3 cloves garlic, minced
- ½ cup butter
- 3 tablespoons soy sauce
- 1 tablespoon dried parsley
- Pepper to taste
- 6 chicken thighs

Step-by-Step Directions

1. Combine garlic, butter, soy sauce, parsley and pepper in a bowl.
2. Add to a pan over medium heat.
3. Simmer until butter is melted.
4. Place chicken in a baking pan.
5. Pour butter mixture over chicken.
6. Transfer chicken to the broil rack inside the Oster Digital French Door Oven.
7. Choose broil setting.
8. Set it to 375 degrees F.
9. Press start.
10. Broil for 20 minutes.

Serving Suggestion: Sprinkle with dried parsley.

Tip: Use skinless chicken for this recipe.

Broiled Lemon Butter Chicken

The combination of lemon juice and butter infuse chicken with incredible flavor.

Prep Time and Cooking Time: 20 minutes | Serves: 4

Ingredients to Use:

- 2 tablespoons lemon juice
- 2 teaspoons lemon zest
- 3 cloves garlic, minced
- 2 tablespoons butter
- Salt and pepper to taste
- 3 lb. chicken
- 1 lemon, sliced

Step-by-Step Directions

1. Add lemon juice, lemon zest, garlic, butter, salt and pepper to a bowl.
2. Mix until paste is formed.
3. Spread lemon mixture on all sides of chicken.
4. Add the chicken to the broil pan inside the Oster Digital French Door Oven.
5. Select broil setting.
6. Set it to 375 degrees F.
7. Broil chicken for 5 minutes per side.
8. Add lemon slices on top of chicken.
9. Broil for 1 minute.

Serving Suggestion: You can also squeeze broiled lemons over chicken.

Tip: You'll get better results with this dish if you don't skin the chicken.

Broiled Sweet Chicken

This broiled chicken is a fusion of sweet and savory flavors.

Prep Time and Cooking Time: 30 minutes | Serves: 4

Ingredients to Use:

- 8 chicken thighs
- 3 cloves garlic, minced
- 2 tablespoons olive oil
- 1 tablespoon apple cider vinegar
- 2 tablespoons soy sauce
- 2 teaspoons Worcestershire sauce
- 1 teaspoon hot sauce
- ½ tablespoon ketchup
- 1 tablespoon brown sugar

Step-by-Step Directions

1. Set your Oster Digital French Door Oven to broil.
2. Preheat it to 375 degrees F.
3. Place chicken in a baking pan.
4. Combine remaining ingredients in a bowl.
5. Brush sauce on both sides of chicken.
6. Transfer chicken to broil rack.
7. Broil chicken for 5 minutes.
8. Brush with remaining sauce, flip and broil for another 5 minutes.
9. Broil until internal temperature reaches 165 degrees F.

Serving Suggestion: Garnish with chopped parsley.

Tip: Use low-sodium soy sauce.

Baked Paprika Chicken Breast

This baked chicken is impressive and simple to make.

Prep Time and Cooking Time: 4o minutes | Serves: 4

Ingredients to Use:

- 4 chicken breast fillets
- 1 tablespoon butter
- ½ teaspoon paprika
- ½ teaspoon garlic powder
- Salt and pepper to taste

Step-by-Step Directions

1. Preheat your Oster Digital French Door Oven to 450 degrees F.
2. Brush chicken with butter.
3. Sprinkle with paprika, garlic powder, salt and pepper.
4. Place chicken inside the oven.
5. Select bake setting.
6. Press start.
7. Bake for 15 minutes.
8. Choose broil setting.
9. Broil for 3 minutes.

Serving Suggestion: Serve with grilled asparagus.

Tip: Flatten chicken with meat mallet.

Chicken Parmesan

Crispy and delicious, this chicken Parmesan is full of delicious flavors you like.

Prep Time and Cooking Time: 40 minutes | Serves: 4

Ingredients to Use:

- 1 egg
- 1 teaspoon garlic powder
- ½ cup Parmesan cheese, grated
- ½ cup breadcrumbs
- Salt and pepper to taste
- 4 chicken breast fillets
- Cooking spray
- 1 cup marinara sauce
- 1 cup mozzarella cheese, shredded

Step-by-Step Directions

1. Select bake setting in your Oster Digital French Door Oven.
2. Preheat it to 450 degrees F.
3. In a bowl, beat egg.
4. In another bowl, mix garlic powder, Parmesan cheese, breadcrumbs, salt and pepper.
5. Spray chicken with oil.

6. Dip in egg and then in the breadcrumb mixture.

7. Place chicken inside the oven.

8. Press start.

9. Bake for 10 minutes per side.

10. Take the chicken out of the oven.

11. Top with the marinara sauce and cheese.

12. Place chicken in the broil rack.

13. Broil for 3 minutes.

Serving Suggestion: Serve with roasted broccoli or cauliflower rice.

Tip: You can also top chicken with chopped basil before broiling.

Stuffed Turkey Breast

This turkey breast is loaded with amazing flavors you can't get enough of.

Prep Time and Cooking Time: 45 minutes | Serves: 4

Ingredients to Use:

- 4 slices bacon
- 1 tablespoon olive oil
- 1 shallot, minced
- ¾ cup mushrooms, chopped
- Salt and pepper to taste
- 4 turkey breast fillets
- ½ cup pesto

Step-by-Step Directions

1. Select bake setting in your Oster Digital French Door Oven.
2. Preheat it to 350 degrees F.
3. In a pan over medium heat, cook bacon slices until crispy.
4. Drain, crumble and set aside.
5. In the same pan, cook shallots and mushrooms for 2 minutes.
6. Season with salt and pepper.
7. Create a pocket in the turkey breast.
8. Stuff with the mushroom mixture, pesto and bacon bits.
9. Season both sides with salt and pepper.
10. Place turkey inside the oven.
11. Bake for 30 minutes.

Serving Suggestion: Serve with sautéed carrots and beets.

Tip: You can also broil chicken for 3 minutes after baking to give it golden finish.

Mediterranean Turkey

Bring home the flavors of Mediterranean region with this simple and delicious turkey recipe.

Prep Time and Cooking Time: 30 minutes | Serves: 4

Ingredients to Use:

- 4 chicken breast fillet
- Salt and pepper to taste
- 3 tablespoons olive oil
- 2 cups cherry tomatoes
- 16 olives, pitted and sliced
- 3 tablespoons capers, drained

Step-by-Step Directions

1. Season both sides of chicken with salt and pepper.
2. Add oil to a pan and cook chicken for 3 minutes per side.
3. Stir in the rest of the ingredients.
4. Transfer chicken mixture to a baking pan.
5. Place it inside the Oster Digital French Door Oven.
6. Select bake setting.
7. Set it to 475 degrees F for 15 minutes.
8. Press start.
9. Wait for cycle to complete.

Serving Suggestion: Serve with fresh green salad.

Tip: Use black olives for this recipe.

Baked Caesar Chicken

You'd love this creamy and delicious baked Caesar chicken that's very easy to make.

Prep Time and Cooking Time: 40 minutes | Serves: 4

Ingredients to Use:

- 4 chicken breast fillets
- ½ cup creamy Caesar salad dressing
- 1 avocado, sliced into cubes
- ¼ cup Parmesan cheese, shredded

Step-by-Step Directions

1. Add chicken to a baking pan.
2. In a bowl, combine the dressing, cheese and avocado.
3. Place it inside the Oster Digital French Door Oven.
4. Select bake function.
5. Set it to 375 degrees F for 30 minutes.
6. Press start.
7. Wait for cycle to complete.

Serving Suggestion: You can also sprinkle with more Parmesan cheese before serving.

Tip: Internal temperature should be at least 170 degrees F.

CHAPTER 5: VEGAN & VEGETARIAN 8 RECIPES

Roasted Veggies

Colorful and vibrant, these roasted veggies are sure to please.

Prep Time and Cooking Time: 40 minutes | Serves: 4

Ingredients to Use:

- Water
- 1 sweet potato, sliced into rounds
- 4 potatoes, sliced into rounds
- 2 carrots, sliced
- 1 beet, sliced into rounds
- 2 cups Brussels sprouts, sliced in half
- 1 cup cabbage, sliced
- 2 cups cauliflower florets
- 1 cup broccolini, sliced
- 1 bell pepper, sliced
- ½ zucchini, sliced into rounds
- 1 tablespoon curry powder
- Salt to taste

Step-by-Step Directions

1. Select bake setting in your Oster Digital French Door Oven.
2. Preheat it to 375 degrees F.

3. Add a pot filled with water to your stovetop.

4. Boil sweet potatoes, potatoes, carrots and beets until tender.

5. Drain and transfer to a baking pan.

6. Blanch the remaining vegetables until tender but still crunchy.

7. Stir into the first batch of veggies.

8. Season with curry powder and salt.

9. Place baking pan inside the oven.

10. Select bake and press start.

11. Bake for 10 minutes.

Serving Suggestion: Serve with tahini.

Tip: You can also drizzle with a little lemon juice before serving.

Veggies with Thyme

Thyme brings out the spectacular flavors of this vegetable medley.

Prep Time and Cooking Time: 45 minutes | Serves: 10

Ingredients to Use:

- 3 cups sweet onion, sliced
- ½ lb. mushrooms, sliced in half
- 1 red bell pepper, sliced
- 1 yellow bell pepper, sliced
- 2 lb. potatoes
- 3 carrots, sliced
- 2 tablespoons olive oil
- 2 tablespoons butter, melted
- 2 tablespoons thyme, minced
- Salt and pepper to taste

Step-by-Step Directions

1. Add vegetables to a baking pan.
2. Stir in the olive oil and butter.
3. Season with thyme, salt and pepper.
4. Select bake setting in your Oster Digital French Door Oven.
5. Add baking pan to the oven.
6. Set temperature to 350 degrees F.
7. Press start.
8. Bake for 45 minutes.
9. Wait for cycle to complete.

Serving Suggestion: Garnish with lemon slices.

Tip: Use button mushrooms for this recipe.

Cheesy Potato

It's hard to say no to a vegetable dish like this one.

Prep Time and Cooking Time: 30 minutes | Serves: 6

Ingredients to Use:

- 3 potatoes

- 1 ½ teaspoons vegetable oil

- ½ cup sour cream

- ½ cup half and half

- ½ cup butter

- ½ cup green onion, sliced

- 1 cup cheddar cheese, shredded

- Pinch paprika

- Salt and pepper to taste

Step-by-Step Directions

1. Coat potatoes with oil.

2. Add potatoes to a baking pan.

3. Place the baking pan inside the Oster Digital French Door Oven.

4. Select bake setting.

5. Set it to 400 degrees F for 50 minutes.

6. Press start.

7. Wait for cycle to complete.

8. Slice the potatoes and scoop out the pulp.

9. Mix the potato flesh with the remaining ingredients.

10. Put mixture back on top of potatoes.

11. Return inside the oven.

12. Set it to 375 degrees F for 20 minutes.

13. Press start.

14. Wait for baking to complete.

Serving Suggestion: Garnish with chopped green onion.

Tip: You can also use Gruyere cheese instead of cheddar.

Vegan Pizza

This pizza will make you go wow whether you're a vegan or not.

Prep Time and Cooking Time: 1 hour | Serves: 8

Ingredients to Use:

- 1 refrigerated vegan pizza crust
- ½ cup marinara sauce
- 1 cup vegan mozzarella cheese
- ½ cup fresh basil leaves, chopped
- Pinch Italian seasoning

Step-by-Step Directions

1. Spread marinara sauce on top of crust.
2. Sprinkle with cheese, basil and Italian seasoning.
3. Place the pizza inside the Oster Digital French Door Oven.
4. Press pizza setting.
5. Set temperature to 375 degrees F.
6. Set time to 20 minutes.
7. Press start button.
8. Wait for cycle to complete.

Serving Suggestion: Let cool before slicing and serving.

Tip: You can also make your own vegan pizza dough if you like.

Dehydrated Celery

Want your celery to last longer? Here's how you can do just that.

Prep Time and Cooking Time: 8 hours and 15 minutes | Serves: 4

Ingredients to Use:

- 8 cups celery, sliced

Step-by-Step Directions

1. Spread the celery slices on top of the dehydrator tray inside the Oster Digital French Door Oven.

2. Choose dehydrate function.

3. Set temperature to 135 degrees F.

4. Set time to 8 hours.

5. Press start.

6. Wait for cycle to finish.

Serving Suggestion: Let cool before serving or storing in airtight container.

Tip: You can also season celery with garlic powder or salt and pepper before dehydrating.

Potato Chips

Make your own potato chips sans the grease and additives.

Prep Time and Cooking Time: 8 hours and 30 minutes | Serves: 8

Ingredients to Use:

- Water

- 2 lb. potatoes, peeled and sliced into thin rounds

- 1 tablespoon salt

Step-by-Step Directions

1. Fill your pot with water.

2. Add potatoes and salt.

3. Bring to a boil.

4. Reduce heat and simmer until potatoes are a little tender.

5. Drain and let cool.

6. Dry with paper towel.

7. Transfer the potatoes to the dehydrator tray of the Oster Digital French Door Oven.

8. Select dehydrate setting.

9. Set temperature to 135 degrees F.

10. Set time to 8 hours.

11. Press start.

12. Wait for cycle to finish.

Serving Suggestion: Serve with your favorite dip.

Tip: Slice the potatoes using a mandolin.

Dehydrated Mushrooms

You'll find so many uses for dehydrated mushrooms and for sure, you'll be delighted when preparing these each time.

Prep Time and Cooking Time: 11 hours and 45 minutes | Serves: 4

Ingredients to Use:

- 8 cups large Portobello mushrooms

- ¼ cup tamari

- 2 tablespoons olive oil

- 1 teaspoon garlic powder

- 1 teaspoon lemon juice

Step-by-Step Directions

1.   Toss mushrooms in a mixture of tamari, olive oil, garlic powder and lemon juice.

2.   Marinate for 40 minutes.

3.   Transfer marinated mushrooms to the dehydrator tray of the Oster Digital French Door Oven.

4.   Press dehydrate function.

5.   Set temperature to 135 degrees F.

6.   Set time to 1 hour.

7.   Press start.

8.   Once cycle is complete, restart the oven.

9.   Press dehydrate setting.

10.   Set temperature to 105 degrees F.

11.   Set time to 10 hours.

12.   Press start. Wait for cycle to complete.

Serving Suggestion: Let cool before serving or storing in airtight container.

Tip: You can grind dehydrated mushrooms and use ground mushrooms as seasoning for your cooking.

Vegetarian Pizza

You don't have to be a vegetarian to enjoy this amazing vegetarian pizza.

Prep Time and Cooking Time: 40 minutes | Serves: 6

Ingredients to Use:

- 1 refrigerated pizza crust
- 1 cup marinara sauce
- 1 teaspoon Italian seasoning
- 1 cup mozzarella cheese, shredded
- 1 cup tomatoes, chopped
- 1 cup black olives, chopped
- 1 cup spinach, steamed and sliced

Step-by-Step Directions

1. Spread marinara sauce on top of pizza crust.
2. Sprinkle with Italian seasoning.
3. Top with cheese, tomatoes, olives and spinach.
4. Place pizza inside the Oster Digital French Door Oven.
5. Choose bake setting.
6. Set temperature to 375 degrees F.
7. Set time to 30 minutes.
8. Press start and wait for cycle to complete.

Serving Suggestion: Sprinkle with Parmesan cheese before serving.

Tip: Extend baking time if you want your pizza crust crispier.

CHAPTER 6: SOUPS, STEWS & BROTHS 8 RECIPES

Baked Veggie Soup

This peasant-style veggie soup is sure to impress everyone at the dinner table.

Prep Time and Cooking Time: 1 hour and 40 minutes | Serves: 8

Ingredients to Use:

- 5 tablespoons olive oil
- 1 lb. potatoes, sliced into rounds
- 10 oz. mushrooms
- 2 zucchini, sliced
- 2 leeks, chopped
- ¼ cup parsley, chopped
- 4 stalks celery, chopped
- 15 oz. canned diced tomatoes
- 6 cups water
- 1 tablespoon Parmesan cheese, grated
- Salt and pepper to taste

Step-by-Step Directions

1. Preheat your Oster Digital French Door Oven to 350 degrees F.
2. Add oil to a small pot over medium heat.
3. Arrange vegetables in layers.

4.   Pour in the tomatoes and water.

5.   Sprinkle with Parmesan cheese, salt and pepper.

6.   Bring to a boil.

7.   Once boiling, transfer pot to the oven.

8.   Select bake setting.

9.   Set it to 1 hour.

10.   Press start button.

11.   Wait for baking to finish.

Serving Suggestion: Garnish with chopped parsley.

Tip: Clean celery thoroughly to ensure they are grit free before using.

Baked Bean Soup

This bean soup is truly comforting. You'll relish every sip.

Prep Time and Cooking Time: 40 minutes | Serves: 14

Ingredients to Use:

- 3 quarts water
- 1 lb. dried navy beans
- 1 ¼ lb. ham, cooked and diced
- 1 cup onion, diced
- 1 cup celery, diced
- 1 cup carrot, diced
- 16 oz. tomato sauce
- 1 teaspoon dried marjoram
- 2 teaspoons chili powder
- Salt and pepper to taste

Step-by-Step Directions

1. Mix all the ingredients in a small pot or baking pan.
2. Place it inside the Oster Digital French Door Oven.
3. Select bake function.
4. Set it to 350 degrees F.
5. Set temperature to 5 hours.
6. Press start.
7. Wait for cycle to complete.

Serving Suggestion: Sprinkle with Parmesan cheese.

Tip: You can also soak dried navy beans for 1 hour in water before using.

Beef & Vegetable Soup

This is hearty beef and veggie soup that you and your family will surely love.

Prep Time and Cooking Time: 2 hours | Serves: 8

Ingredients to Use:

- 1 tablespoon olive oil
- 1 ½ lb. beef sirloin, sliced into cubes
- 1 onion, chopped
- 3 ribs celery, chopped
- 28 oz. beef broth
- 4 cups water
- 10 baby carrot, sliced into cubes
- 2 potatoes, sliced into cubes
- 14 oz. canned diced tomatoes
- 2 bay leaves
- 2 teaspoons hot pepper sauce
- 2 teaspoons garlic powder
- 1 cup green beans
- 1 cup corn kernels

Step-by-Step Directions

1. Pour oil into a pot over medium heat.
2. Cook beef until browned on all sides.
3. Transfer to a plate.
4. Add onion and celery to the pot.
5. Cook for 3 to 5 minutes.

6. Put the beef back to the pot along with the rest of the ingredients except corn.

7. Bring to a boil.

8. Once boiling, transfer to a baking pan and place inside the Oster Digital French Door Oven.

9. Press bake setting.

10. Set temperature to 350 degrees F.

11. Set time to 30 minutes.

12. Press start.

13. Wait for cycle to complete.

14. Stir in corn kernels and heat in the stove for 5 minutes before serving.

Serving Suggestion: Garnish with fresh herbs.

Tip: Trim fat from the beef before using.

Chicken Soup

This is the kind of comforting soup that will instantly brighten up your day.

Prep Time and Cooking Time: 2 hours and 30 minutes | Serves: 6

Ingredients to Use:

- 2 onions, sliced

- 7 carrots, peeled

- 2 sticks celery, sliced

- 1 rutabaga, peeled and sliced

- 2 leeks, sliced

- 1 lb. chicken, sliced into chunks

- 1 quart water

- 6 cups chicken broth

Step-by-Step Directions

1. Preheat your Oster Digital French Door Oven to 300 degrees F.

2. Select bake setting.

3. Add all the ingredients to a pot.

4. Bring to a boil over medium high heat.

5. Cook for 30 minutes.

6. After this, carefully transfer soup to a baking pan.

7. Add baking pan to the oven.

8. Set time for 2 hours.

9. Press start.

10. Wait for cycle to finish.

Serving Suggestion: Sprinkle with pepper before serving.

Tip: You can also use baby carrots for this recipe.

Baked Pumpkin Soup

Creamy and savory, this pumpkin soup will entice you to no end.

Prep Time and Cooking Time: 1 hour and 10 minutes | Serves: 6

Ingredients to Use:

- 3 ½ lb. pumpkin, sliced
- 2 teaspoons olive oil
- 3 cups water, divided
- 1 ½ cups dry white wine
- ¼ cup butter
- Salt and pepper to taste

Step-by-Step Directions

1. Preheat your Oster Digital French Door Oven to 450 degrees F.
2. Select bake setting.
3. Set time to 45 minutes.
4. Add the pumpkin slices to a baking pan.
5. Drizzle with oil.
6. Place baking pan inside the oven.
7. Press start.
8. Wait for cycle to complete.
9. Once complete, transfer pumpkin to a food processor.
10. Process until smooth.

11.   Transfer pureed pumpkin to a pot over medium heat.

12.   Stir in the rest of the ingredients.

13.   Bring to a boil and then reduce heat.

14.   Simmer for 30 minutes.

Serving Suggestion: Sprinkle with pumpkin seeds.

Tip: You can also season pumpkin slices with salt and pepper before baking in the oven.

Cauliflower Soup

You'll love how creamy, delicious and easy to make this cauliflower soup is.

Prep Time and Cooking Time: 1 hour and 10 minutes | Serves: 4

Ingredients to Use:

- 2 lb. cauliflower florets
- 2 tablespoons olive oil
- 4 cups vegetable broth
- 1 teaspoon garlic powder
- 2 tablespoons butter
- Salt and pepper to taste

Step-by-Step Directions

1. Preheat your oven to 425 degrees F.
2. Toss cauliflower in oil.
3. Add these to a baking pan.
4. Place baking pan inside the Oster Digital French Door Oven.
5. Set oven to bake.
6. Set time to 35 minutes.
7. Press start.
8. Once cycle is complete, transfer cauliflower to a plate and let cool.
9. Transfer to a food processor.
10. Stir in the rest of the ingredients.

11.   Process until smooth.

12.   Transfer pureed soup to a pot over medium heat.

13.   Heat through before serving.

Serving Suggestion: Garnish with parsley.

Tip: You can make this soup ahead of time and freeze until ready to serve.

Sweet Potato Soup

Relish every sip of this wonderful and delicious sweet potato soup.

Prep Time and Cooking Time: 40 minutes | Serves: 4

Ingredients to Use:

- 4 cups sweet potato, sliced into cubes
- 1 tablespoon olive oil
- 1 teaspoon garlic powder
- Salt and pepper to taste
- 4 cups vegetable broth

Step-by-Step Directions

1. Toss sweet potato in oil.
2. Arrange the sweet potatoes in a baking pan.
3. Place baking pan inside the Oster Digital French Door Oven.
4. Select bake setting.
5. Set temperature to 425 degrees F.
6. Set time to 30 minutes.
7. Press start.
8. Once cycle is complete, cool sweet potatoes in a plate.
9. Transfer to a food processor.
10. Process until pureed.
11. Put it in a baking pan.

12. Stir in the rest of the ingredients.

13. Place the baking pan inside the oven.

14. Press warm setting.

15. Press start.

16. Wait for cycle to complete.

Serving Suggestion: Garnish with chopped green onions.

Roasted Carrot Soup

This roasted carrot soup will make your dinner more memorable.

Prep Time and Cooking Time: 50 minutes | Serves: 12

Ingredients to Use:

- 4 cups carrots, chopped
- 1 tablespoons olive oil
- 4 cups vegetable broth
- 2 tablespoons butter
- 1 teaspoon garlic powder
- 1 teaspoon ground nutmeg
- Salt and pepper to taste

Step-by-Step Directions

1. Coat carrots with olive oil.
2. Spread carrots in a baking pan.
3. Place baking pan inside the Oster Digital French Door Oven.
4. Set temperature to 425 degrees F.
5. Set time to 30 minutes.
6. Press start.
7. Once cycle is complete, let carrots cool in a plate.
8. Place carrots in a food processor.
9. Puree until smooth.

10.   Add to a pot.

11.   Stir in the rest of the ingredients.

12.   Place pot over medium heat.

13.   Bring to a boil and then simmer for 10 minutes.

Serving Suggestion: Garnish with carrot slices.

Tip: Use freshly ground nutmeg.

CHAPTER 7: BEANS & EGGS 8 RECIPES

Boston Baked Beans

Here's how you can make the classic Boston baked beans.

Prep Time and Cooking Time: 5 hours | Serves: 6

Ingredients to Use:

- 2 cups navy beans, soaked overnight in water

- 1 onion, chopped

- ½ lb. bacon

- 3 tablespoons molasses

- ½ cup ketchup

- ¼ teaspoon dry mustard

- ¼ cup brown sugar

- 1 tablespoon Worcestershire sauce

- Salt and pepper to taste

Step-by-Step Directions

1. Add beans and water to a pot over medium heat.

2. Simmer for 2 hours.

3. Drain and set aside cooking liquid.

4. Preheat your Oster Digital French Door Oven to 325 degrees F.

5. Spread beans in a baking pan.

6. Layer onion and bacon on top.

7. In a pan over medium heat, add reserved cooking liquid along with the rest of the ingredients.

8. Pour this over the beans.

9. Cover the baking pan with foil.

10. Add baking pan to the oven.

11. Set it to bake.

12. Set it to 4 hours.

13. Press start.

14. Wait for cycle to complete.

Serving Suggestion: Serve with cornbread and honey.

Tip: You can also use turkey bacon for this recipe.

Sugar Baked Pork & Beans

These baked beans are smoky and savory. You can't get enough of it.

Prep Time and Cooking Time: 2 hours and 30 minutes | Serves: 8

Ingredients to Use:

- 10 slices bacon, chopped and cooked crispy

- 1 tablespoon olive oil

- 1 yellow onion, chopped

- ½ green bell pepper, chopped

- 54 oz. canned pork and beans

- 4 tablespoons ketchup

- ¼ cup molasses

- 2/3 cup brown sugar

- ¼ cup vinegar

- 2 teaspoons dry mustard

Step-by-Step Directions

1. Preheat your Oster Digital French Door Oven to 325 degrees F.

2. In a pan over medium heat, pour oil and cook onion and bell pepper for 5 minutes.

3. Stir in the remaining ingredients.

4. Simmer for 5 minutes.

5. Add bean mixture to a baking pan.

6. Place bacon on top.

7. Place baking pan inside the Oster Digital French Door Oven.

8. Set time to 3 hours.

9. Press start.

10. Wait for cycle to complete.

Serving Suggestion: Let sit for 5 minutes before serving.

Tip: Use cider vinegar.

Cheesy Eggs

These baked eggs are a great hit each time.

Prep Time and Cooking Time: 50 minutes | Serves: 8

Ingredients to Use:

- 1 tablespoon butter

- 12 eggs, beaten

- 16 oz. cottage cheese

- 16 oz. Pepper Jack cheese, shredded

- ½ cup all-purpose flour

- Salt to taste

Step-by-Step Directions

1. Brush your baking pan with butter.

2. In a bowl, whisk together all the remaining ingredients.

3. Pour mixture into the baking pan.

4. Place it inside the Oster Digital French Door Oven.

5. Set temperature to 350 degrees.

6. Set time to 50 minutes.

7. Press start.

8. Wait for cycle to complete.

Serving Suggestion: Serve with sour cream and garnish with green onions.

Tip: You can also use cheddar cheese instead of Pepper Jack cheese.

Ham & Cheese Egg Bake

Cheesy, savory and healthy—there's nothing more you can ask from this egg bake.

Prep Time and Cooking Time: 50 minutes | Serves: 12

Ingredients to Use:

- 8 eggs, beaten
- 1 ¾ cups milk
- 4 ½ oz. mushrooms, sliced
- ½ cup sweet red pepper, chopped
- ¼ cup green onions, sliced
- 2 cups ham, cooked and diced
- 2 tablespoons butter
- 2 tablespoons parsley, chopped
- ½ teaspoon dried basil
- Salt and pepper to taste
- 3 cups mozzarella cheese, shredded
- 3 cups cheddar cheese, shredded

Step-by-Step Directions

1. Preheat your Oster Digital French Door Oven to 350 degrees F.
2. Select bake setting.

3.   In a baking pan, mix eggs, milk, mushrooms, red bell pepper, green onions, ham, butter, parsley, basil, salt and pepper.

4.   Top with the cheeses.

5.   Place baking pan inside the oven.

6.   Set it to 40 minutes.

7.   Press start.

8.   Wait for cycle to complete.

Serving Suggestion: Let sit for 10 minutes before slicing and serving.

Tip: Use whole milk for best results.

Bacon & Cheese Egg Bake

Everything's better with bacon, right? Here's another recipe to prove this is right.

Prep Time and Cooking Time: 30 minutes | Serves: 4

Ingredients to Use:

- Cooking spray
- 4 eggs
- 4 tablespoons milk
- 2 tablespoons cheddar cheese, shredded
- 2 bacon strips, cooked crisp and crumbled
- 2 teaspoons parsley, minced
- Salt and pepper to taste

Step-by-Step Directions

1. Spray 4 ramekins with oil.
2. Break egg into each ramekin.
3. Pour milk on top of egg.
4. Sprinkle with cheese, bacon, parsley, salt and pepper.
5. Place ramekins inside the Oster Digital French Door Oven.
6. Choose bake setting.
7. Set temperature to 325 degrees.
8. Set time to 15 minutes.
9. Press start.
10. Wait for cycle to complete.

Serving Suggestion: Let cool for 5 minutes before serving.

Tip: You can also use turkey bacon or chopped sausage for this recipe.

Creamy Eggs

Delightful and truly satisfying, these creamy eggs will entice you every time.

Prep Time and Cooking Time: 30 minutes | Serves: 8

Ingredients to Use:

- ¼ cup half and half
- 8 eggs
- 1 cup cheddar cheese, shredded
- 2 tablespoons Parmesan cheese, grated
- Salt and pepper to taste

Step-by-Step Directions

1. Select bake setting in your Oster Digital French Door Oven.
2. Set it to 400 degrees F and preheat it for 5 minutes.
3. Spread half and half in a baking pan.
4. Break eggs on top.
5. Sprinkle cheeses, salt and pepper on top.
6. Place baking pan inside the oven.
7. Bake in the oven for 10 minutes.

Serving Suggestion: Garnish with green onions.

Tip: You can also use all purpose cream instead of half and half.

Egg & Ham

The fact that it's delicious and a cinch to prepare is more than enough reason to prepare this dish more often.

Prep Time and Cooking Time: 30 minutes | Serves: 4

Ingredients to Use:

- ¼ cup croutons
- 2 tablespoons ham, cooked and chopped
- 1 tablespoon butter, melted
- 2 eggs
- 1 tablespoon cheddar cheese, shredded

Step-by-Step Directions

1. Combine ham, croutons and butter in a baking pan.
2. Break eggs on top.
3. Sprinkle cheese on top.
4. Select bake setting in your Oster Digital French Door Oven.
5. Place baking pan inside the oven.
6. Set it to 350 degrees F for 15 minutes.
7. Press start.
8. Wait for cycle to complete.

Serving Suggestion: Serve with fresh fruits.

Tip: Use unsalted butter.

Baked Pork & Beans with Mustard

Description

Prep Time and Cooking Time: 1 hour and 40 minutes | Serves: 12

Ingredients to Use:

- 56 oz. canned pork and beans
- 1 ½ cups brown sugar
- ½ lb. bacon, cooked crispy and crumbled
- 1 cup onion, chopped
- 1 cup soda
- 1 cup ketchup
- 2 tablespoons ground mustard

Step-by-Step Directions

1. Select bake setting in your Oster Digital French Door Oven.
2. Set temperature to 325 degrees F.
3. Combine all the ingredients in a baking pan.
4. Place the baking pan inside the oven.
5. Set time to 1 hour and 30 minutes.
6. Press start.
7. Wait for cycle to complete.

Serving Suggestion: Sprinkle with a little pepper before serving.

Tip: Use pure navy beans if you want to omit pork.

CHAPTER 8: DESSERTS & SNACKS 8 RECIPES

Walnut & Zucchini Muffin

This is the kind of dessert that you definitely can't say no to.

Prep Time and Cooking Time: 40 minutes | Serves: 1 dozen

Ingredients to Use:

- ¾ cup whole wheat flour
- 1 cup all-purpose flour
- 2 teaspoons baking powder
- ¾ teaspoon ground cinnamon
- 2/3 cup brown sugar
- ½ teaspoon salt
- 2 eggs, beaten
- ¾ cup milk
- 1 cup walnuts, chopped
- 1 cup zucchini, shredded
- ½ cup melted butter
- ½ cup raisins

Step-by-Step Directions

1. Choose bake setting in your Oster Digital French Door Oven.
2. Set it to 375 degrees F.
3. Preheat for 10 minutes.

4.   In a bowl, combine all the ingredients.

5.   Pour mixture into muffin pan.

6.   Place muffin pan inside the oven.

7.   Set time to 20 minutes.

8.   Press start to initiate baking cycle.

9.   Let cool for 5 minutes before serving.

Serving Suggestion: Serve with milk.

Tip: You can freeze cooled baked muffins and reheat by pressing warm setting in the oven before serving.

Thyme Crackers

Season your crackers with salt and thyme for a delightful snack.

Prep Time and Cooking Time: 30 minutes | Serves: 80 pieces

Ingredients to Use:

- 2 ½ cups all-purpose flour
- ½ cup whole wheat flour
- 1 teaspoon salt
- ¾ cup water
- ¼ cup olive oil
- 2 tablespoons fresh thyme, minced
- Salt to taste

Step-by-Step Directions

1. Combine all the ingredients in a bowl.
2. Knead dough and divide into 3 portions.
3. Roll out each portion into a thin dough.
4. Cut using cookie cutter.
5. Place these in a baking pan.
6. Set the baking pan inside the Oster Digital French Door Oven.
7. Select bake function.
8. Set it to 325 degrees F for 12 minutes.
9. Press start and then wait for baking to complete.

Serving Suggestion: Sprinkle with a little bit of salt before serving.

Tip: You can also use dried thyme if fresh is not available.

Cauliflower Breadsticks

Cheesy and full of flavor, these breadsticks will always be a hit at any party.

Prep Time and Cooking Time: 50 minutes | Serves: 12

Ingredients to Use:

- 6 cups cauliflower florets
- ½ cup mozzarella cheese, shredded
- ½ cup Parmesan cheese, grated
- ½ cup cheddar cheese, shredded
- 1 egg
- ¼ cup basil, chopped
- ¼ cup fresh parsley, chopped
- 1 clove garlic, minced
- Salt and pepper to taste

Step-by-Step Directions

1. Select bake function in your Oster Digital French Door Oven.
2. Set it to 425 degrees F.
3. Preheat for 15 minutes.
4. Put cauliflower in a food processor.
5. Pulse until finely ground.
6. Microwave cauliflower rice for 8 minutes.
7. Squeeze dry with paper towel.
8. Place in a bowl.

9.   Stir in the rest of the ingredients.

10.   Spread mixture in a baking pan.

11.   Set oven to bake.

12.   Set time to 25 minutes.

13.   Press start.

14.   Wait for cycle to end.

15.   Slice into sticks.

Serving Suggestion: Serve with marinara sauce.

Tip: You can also use prepared cauliflower rice for this recipe.

Yogurt Cornbread

There's so much fluffy goodness in this delicious yogurt cornbread.

Prep Time and Cooking Time: 30 minutes | Serves: 8

Ingredients to Use:

- 1 cup yellow cornmeal
- ¼ cup all-purpose flour
- 2 teaspoons baking powder
- Pinch salt
- ¼ teaspoon baking soda
- 1 egg, beaten
- 1 cup yogurt
- ½ cup milk
- ¼ cup vegetable oil
- 1 tablespoon honey

Step-by-Step Directions

1. Mix all the ingredients in a bowl.
2. Pour mixture into a baking pan.
3. Select bake function in your Oster Digital French Door Oven.
4. Set it to 425 degrees F.
5. Place the baking pan inside the oven.
6. Set time to 20 minutes.
7. Press start.
8. Wait for cycle to finish.

Serving Suggestion: Let cool before slicing and serving.

Tip: You can also add nuts to the mixture.

Roasted Pumpkin Seeds

Want a snack that's healthy but delicious? Here's one that you'd definitely want to try.

Prep Time and Cooking Time: 1 hour | Serves: 2 cups

Ingredients to Use:

- 2 cups pumpkin seeds
- 1 teaspoon Worcestershire sauce
- 5 teaspoons melted butter
- 1 teaspoon sugar
- ¼ teaspoon cayenne pepper
- ¼ teaspoon garlic powder
- ½ teaspoon salt

Step-by-Step Directions

1. Combine all the ingredients in a baking pan.
2. Place baking pan inside the Oster Digital French Door Oven.
3. Select bake function.
4. Set temperature to 250 degrees F.
5. Set time to 1 hour.
6. Press start.
7. Wait for cycle to end.

Serving Suggestion: Let cool before serving.

Tip: Omit cayenne pepper if you don't want your seeds spicy.

Rosemary Walnuts

You'll surely enjoy snacking on these rosemary walnuts.

Prep Time and Cooking Time: 20 minutes | Serves: 2 cups

Ingredients to Use:

- 2 cups walnuts, sliced in half
- Cooking spray
- 2 teaspoons dried rosemary
- Salt to taste

Step-by-Step Directions

1. Spray walnuts with oil.
2. Sprinkle with rosemary and salt.
3. Add these to a baking pan.
4. Place the baking pan inside the Oster Digital French Door Oven.
5. Choose bake setting.
6. Set it to 350 degrees F for 10 minutes.
7. Press start.
8. Wait for cycle to complete.

Serving Suggestion: Let cool before serving.

Tip: Add cayenne pepper to the mixture if you want your walnuts spicy.

Herbed Bread

Herbs make regular bread a lot more special.

Prep Time and Cooking Time: 55 minutes | Serves: 1 loaf

Ingredients to Use:

- 3 cups all-purpose flour
- 1 tablespoon baking powder
- 3 tablespoons sugar
- 3 teaspoons caraway seeds
- ½ teaspoon dried thyme
- ½ teaspoon ground nutmeg
- ½ teaspoon salt
- 1/3 cup canola oil
- 1 cup milk
- 1 egg, beaten

Step-by-Step Directions

1. Combine all the ingredients in a bowl.
2. Pour mixture into a loaf pan.
3. Place the loaf pan inside the Oster Digital French Door Oven.
4. Choose bake setting.
5. Set it to 350 degrees F for 50 minutes.
6. Press start.
7. Wait for cycle to end.

Serving Suggestion: Serve with fruit jam.

Tip: Use fat-free milk.

Choco Peanut Butter Cookies

These sweet treat will send your sweet tooth to heaven.

Prep Time and Cooking Time: 30 minutes | Serves: 3 ½ dozen

Ingredients to Use:

- 32 oz. chocolate fudge frosting
- 1 egg
- 1 cup peanut butter
- 1 ½ cups all-purpose flour
- 1 cup sugar

Step-by-Step Directions

1. Combine all the ingredients except frosting in a bowl.
2. Mix well.
3. Drop spoonfuls of the mixture on top of a baking pan.
4. Flatten with a fork.
5. Place baking pan inside the Oster Digital French Door Oven.
6. Select bake setting.
7. Set it to 375 degrees F for 10 minutes.
8. Press start.
9. Top with frosting and serve.

Serving Suggestion: You can also top with candy sprinkles.

Tip: Use chunky peanut butter.

APPENDIX : RECIPES INDEX

9 781802 443370